918.1

FOCUS ON
BRAZIL

Brian Dicks

Evans Brothers Limited

Published by Evans Brothers Limited
2A Portman Mansions
Chiltern Street
London W1M 1LE

© Evans Brothers Limited 1995

First published in Great Britain in 1995

Editor Karen Ball
Managing Editor Su Swallow
Designer Sally Boothroyd
Map by Jillian Luff of Bitmap Graphics

Printed in Hong Kong by Dah Hua Printing Co. Ltd

ISBN 0 237 51439 7

Acknowledgements
The author and publishers would like to thank the following for
permission to reproduce the photographs: Bruce Coleman 4; Mary
Evans Picture Library 6 (right); Robert Harding 13, 21, 22, 26, 28,
29, 30, 31; The Hutchison Library 8, 10, 14, 17, 20; The Image
Bank 6 (left), 11, 19; Imagenlatina 13, 21; South American
Pictures 9, 11, 15 (top and right), 18, 25 (top), 27 (top); Spectrum
7, 9, 10, 12, 25 (bottom), 27 (bottom), 29; Trip 15 (left), 16, 20
(right), 23, 31 (left)

Cover The figure of Christ on the summit of
Corcovado, overlooking Rio de Janeiro

Title page The scarlet macaw is one of thousands
of animals that inhabit the Amazon jungle.

Opposite The mountain ranges of northeast
Brazil provide some of the country's most
dramatic scenery.

Contents

Introducing Brazil

A Huge Country

The people of Brazil often say they live in a 'continent' rather than a 'country'. This is because nearly half the continent of South America belongs to Brazil. Brazil is the world's fifth largest country. It has over 8 $^1/_2$ million sq kms of land, making it almost 35 times bigger than the United Kingdom. The distance across Brazil is greater than the distance between London and Moscow.

The people

With over 155 million people, Brazil is also the world's fifth largest country in population. Some parts of Brazil are overcrowded, whereas other areas have very few people. Most of the Brazilian population lives along the Atlantic coast where there are large cities, such as Salvador, Rio de Janeiro and Pôrto Alegre.

The Brazilians are a mixture of many peoples, in particular native Indians (Amerindians), Negroes (originally from West Africa) and Europeans, especially Portuguese. These and other peoples make Brazil a multi-racial country. The national language is Portuguese but it sounds different to the language of Portugal, just as American English sounds different to British English.

A Federal Republic

Brazil's official name in Portuguese is República Federativa do Brasil, meaning the 'Federal Republic of Brazil'. It is made up of 26 States and the Federal District of Brasília, the country's capital. Each state has a Governor and Assembly (Parliament), but all national decisions are taken by the Federal Government in Brasília. The National Congress is divided into the Senate and the Chamber of Deputies, rather like Britain's Houses of Lords and Commons. Brazil's head of state is the President who appoints a Cabinet of Ministers to help with his work.

Brazil's famous Amazon jungle

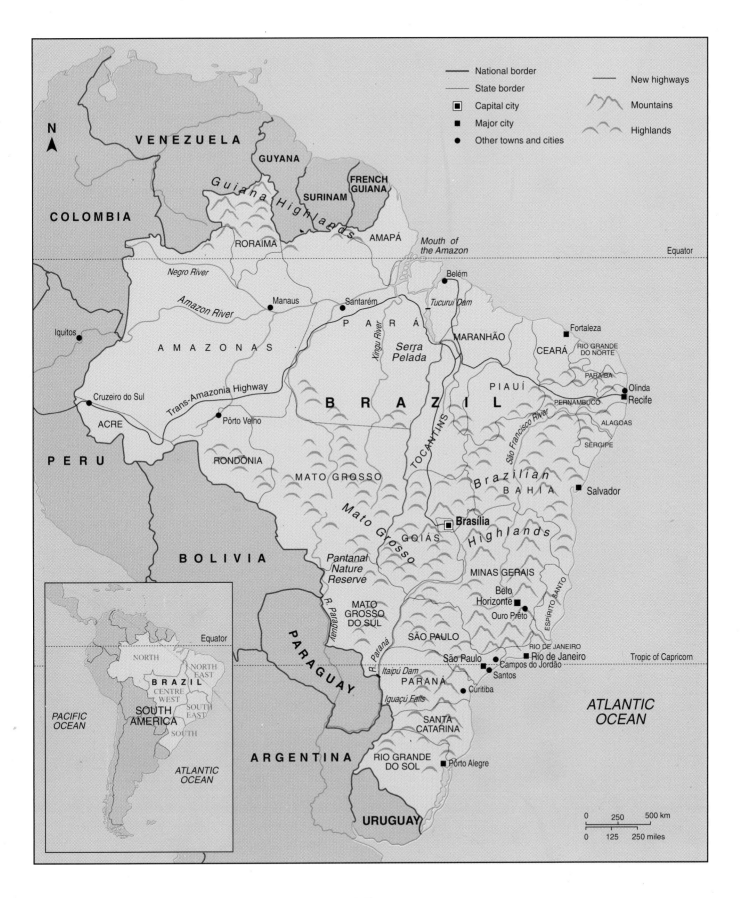

N

VENEZUELA

COLOMBIA

GUYANA

SURINAM

FRENCH
GUIANA

Guiana Highlands

RORAIMA

AMAPÁ

Mouth
of the Amazon

Equator

Negro River

Belém

Amazon River

Manaus

Santarém

Tucuruí Dam

Fortaleza

Iquitos

P A R Á

MARANHÃO

CEARÁ

RIO GRANDE
DO NORTE

A M A Z O N A S

Xingu River

Serra
Pelada

PIAUÍ

PARAÍBA

Olinda
Recife

Cruzeiro do Sul

Trans-Amazonia Highway

B R A Z I L

PERNAMBUCO

ALAGOAS

ACRE

São Francisco River

SÉRGIPE

Pôrto Velho

TOCANTINS

PERU

RONDÔNIA

Brazilian

BAHIA

Salvador

MATO GROSSO

Mato Grosso

Highlands

Brasília

BOLIVIA

GOIÁS

Pantanal
Nature
Reserve

MINAS GERAIS

R. Paraguay

MATO
GROSSO
DO SUL

Belo
Horizonte

ESPÍRITO SANTO

Ouro Prêto

SÃO PAULO

RIO DE JANEIRO

Tropic of Capricorn

PARAGUAY

R. Paraná

São Paulo

Rio de Janeiro

Campos do Jordão

Santos

R. Itaipú Dam

PARANÁ

Cúritiba

ATLANTIC
OCEAN

Iguaçú Falls

PACIFIC
OCEAN

NORTH

NORTH
EAST

BRAZIL

CENTRE
WEST

SOUTH
EAST

SOUTH
AMERICA

SOUTH

ATLANTIC
OCEAN

Equator

SANTA
CATARINA

ARGENTINA

RIO GRANDE
DO SOL

Pôrto Alegre

URUGUAY

National border
State border
□ Capital city
■ Major city
● Other towns and cities

New highways
Mountains
Highlands

0   250   500 km

0   125   250 miles

History and exploration

In the 15th century Portugal and Spain were responsible for much of the exploration and mapping of South America. When explorers from Portugal and Spain arrived in Brazil, both countries were eager to claim ownership of a country rich in natural resources. Ignoring the birthrights of the native Indians, they signed the Treaty of Tordessilas in 1494 which divided the continent between them.

A Portuguese colony

The first major exploration of Brazil began in 1500 when the Portuguese navigator, Pedro Alvares Cabral, landed near Recife, and claimed the coast for Portugal. Soon

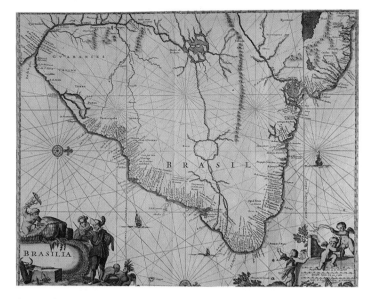

A 16th-century map

Monte Serrat fort in old Salvador

people arrived from mainland Portugal and the islands of Madeira and the Azores. In 1549 Brazil became a Portuguese Colony with a Governor appointed from Lisbon.

The Colony's first capital was Salvador. It grew rapidly as a port, exporting Brazil's valuable products. Rich colonial churches and old merchant mansions from this time are preserved as national monuments.

Sugar and slaves

The Portuguese found a country thinly peopled by native Indians. They were not accustomed to strangers, and felt threatened by the new arrival of Europeans into their country. Although the Indians tried to defend themselves and their land, as more Portuguese settled the Indians were forced to work as slaves.

Slave labour was used in the cutting of brasilwood (see box) and later with sugar-cane when it was introduced to the northeast from Madeira. Negro slaves were shipped from West Africa to work on the large plantations. Around 10 million arrived in Brazil before slavery was finally abolished. Their descendants are an important element in modern Brazil's colourful mix of peoples.

The Bandeirantes

When gold and diamonds were discovered in the Brazilian Highlands, people moved from the coast to the interior. Most were groups of adventurers called 'bandeirantes', after the banner they carried with them. Although searching for riches, each group usually had a priest who founded Christian missions and tried to convert the native Indians to Christianity.

The bandeirantes pushed Brazil's borders far beyond those agreed by the Treaty of Tordessilas. These prospectors supplied the geographical information needed to fill the many blank areas on Brazil's map. Rio de Janeiro was one of the gateways from the Atlantic to the interior. It grew rich as the port sending gold and other valuables to Portugal, and in 1763 it replaced Salvador as Brazil's capital.

Independence

When Napoleon Bonaparte invaded Portugal in 1807, King João IV escaped with his family to Brazil. He made Rio de Janeiro the capital of the entire Portuguese Empire. Returning to Portugal, he left Brazil in the charge of his son Pedro who, in 1822, declared himself Emperor Pedro I of an independent Brazil. During the reign of his son, Pedro II, Brazil became a prosperous country. Many Germans, Italians and other Europeans settled in the southeast and south. Many of them grew coffee on plantations and ran farms of crops and animals. The landlords and the army were unhappy under the rule of Pedro II. By 1889 they were successful and powerful enough to take control themselves, overthrowing Pedro and declaring Brazil a Republic.

Brazil has many beautiful colonial buildings.

Terra do Brasil

The name 'Brazil' comes from the Latin word brasilium. This is a red dye-wood, once imported into Rome from the East. Large supplies of a similar wood were found in Brazil by European explorers. The Indians used it for many purposes, especially for painting their bodies. It was soon sent to Europe as a valuable dye-wood, and the country was called 'terra do brasil', meaning land of the red dye-wood.

The regions

As well as its States, Brazil is also divided into five large regions. These help in the country's government and planning. The regions are the North, Northeast, Centre West, Southeast and South (see map). They vary in size and have different geography, history and modern problems.

The North

This is Brazil's largest, but least populated region. It covers almost half of the country, and most of it belongs to the huge lowland area of Amazonia (see page 10). Covered by a vast equatorial forest (selva), much of it is still inaccessible and little known.

Early European explorers came to this isolated region in search of 'El Dorado', and many never returned. Roraima is said to be the setting of Arthur Conan Doyle's great adventure story, *The Lost World*.

The Northeast

South of Amazonia is another huge area, called the Brazilian Highlands. Its mountain ranges (serras) and high plateau land (planalto) stretch from Bolivia and Paraguay to the Atlantic Ocean. Here a narrow coastal plain, where most Brazilians live, follows the coast from Fortaleza in the north to Pôrto Alegre in the south.

The Northeast was the first part of the

Semi-desert covers much of the Northeast of Brazil.

country to be settled but, today, it is one of Brazil's poorest regions. Away from the coast the countryside is dry, and years can pass without any rainfall. The longest drought in recent times lasted for five years. There are large areas of semi-desert, called 'sertão', where only thorny scrub (caatinga) can grow.

Yet the Northeast also has large and beautiful beaches, a hot and sunny climate, historic towns and cities, and a colourful folklore based on African traditions.

The Centre West

This is Brazil's second largest region. Much of it is 'planalto', with rivers flowing either north to the Amazon or south to the Paraná-Paraguay. The region is also called the 'Mato Grosso', named after its thick scrub-forest. It is another empty part of Brazil, but has some large cattle ranches in its 'cerrado' (grassland) areas. The new capital, Brasília, was built to attract people to this region (see page 13).

Along the borders with Bolivia and Paraguay is the Pantanal Nature Reserve. During the rainy season (October to March) the Paraguay river and its tributaries flood and form a huge wetland of lakes and islands. There are hundreds of freshwater fish, birds and mammals. It is home to flesh-eating piranhas, and the world's largest rodent called 'capybara'. It looks like a guinea pig, but is the size of a farm pig.

The Southeast

The Southeast covers only one tenth of Brazil's area, yet it is the country's most important region. It has the three largest

São Paulo is one of the world's largest cities.

cities, half of Brazil's population and is the main industrial area for Brazil. All this is shared between the States of São Paulo, Rio de Janeiro, Minas Gerais and Espírito Santo. This is also a rich agricultural region where coffee and other profitable crops are grown.

The South

This is Brazil's smallest region, with only eight per cent of the country's land area. Also, it is the only part of Brazil lying outside the Tropics. The cooler climate attracted many European settlers to its

The spectacular Iguaçú Falls

forests, mountains and grasslands. German and Italian peoples are responsible for its vineyards and wine industry. Large cattle ranches are found in the west, and the pine forests support a timber industry. Where the State of Paraná borders Paraguay and Argentina are two of the world's most remarkable water features; the massive Itaipú Dam (see page 21) and the Iguaçú Falls. It is said that at peak flow, enough water tumbles over these falls to fill more than six Olympic-sized swimming pools every second!

Amazonia

The mighty river

Everything about the Amazon River is big. The main river and its many tributaries provide 20 per cent of the world's supply of fresh, running water. This drainage basin is four times larger than Africa's Zaire, and eleven times bigger than the Mississippi. Of the world's twenty largest rivers, ten are in the Amazon basin.

From its source in the Andes of Peru to the Atlantic, the length of the Amazon is 6,762 kilometres. The river reaches the ocean in a huge 'delta' made up of many muddy channels and islands. This delta is 350 kilometres wide, the distance between London and Paris.

The forest is home to native Indians.

Wildlife

Amazonia is the world's largest equatorial forest (selva), and most of it is in Brazil. High temperatures and heavy rainfall make it a natural greenhouse all year round. Hundreds of different plant species are found in the forest, including valuable tropical hardwoods and the rubber tree.

Often called 'inferno verde' (green hell), the selva is home to a huge number of animals, such as wild cats and monkeys, the tapir, sloth, armadillo, alligator and many snakes. Its rivers have more than 40 per cent of the world's freshwater fish. Over 300 different sorts of humming-bird have been recorded, and 1000s of insects have been catalogued.

Amazonia is a vast area of water and forest.

The Indians

As well as unique plants and animals, people also live in the Amazon forest. Over the centuries the native Indians have adapted to its harsh environment. Their houses and furniture are made from forest wood, leaves are used for thatching, and all are held together by lianas (forest creepers). The Indians hunt, fish and collect the fruits of the forest. They also grow yams, manioc and maize.

When the European explorers came, there were probably 15 million Indians in the whole of Amazonia. By 1900 their number had fallen to 4 million. Today, only 120,000 Indians live in Brazil's part of Amazonia. Over the centuries they have been killed by settlers moving in from the coast in search of gold, valuable wood and other riches. Death has also been caused by Western diseases, against which the Indians have no protection. They are still under threat by people who want their land for ranches, roads and timber.

The new El Dorado

Since 1980, there has been another Brazilian 'Gold Rush', this time in Amazonia. Thousands of 'garimpeiros' (gold panners) have moved in, disturbing the Indians and polluting the rivers. However, the biggest danger to the forest comes from the huge cattle ranches. Enormous areas of forest are being cleared for pastureland. This is now a world problem, as the loss of trees is contributing to the 'greenhouse effect'.

The Weeping Tree

The Indians discovered many valuable plants, especially the rubber tree, which grows naturally in the forest. Columbus noted how they made rubber from the gum (latex) of the tree. They called it 'Cahucha', the tree that weeps.

In the 19th century, experiments showed how rubber could be used for making vehicle tyres and many other products. This started a rubber boom in Amazonia, and Manaus became a rich rubber centre.

The boom ended when huge rubber plantations were developed in Malaysia and Sri Lanka (then Ceylon). These plantations were grown from rubber seeds smuggled out of Amazonia, and first grown in London's Kew Gardens. Brazil's natural rubber production was unable to compete.

There are still some rubber tappers in Amazonia however, and special reserves have been set up by the government.

Large areas of the forest are burned for ranches.

The cities

The two biggest cities in Brazil are Rio de Janeiro and São Paulo, with official populations of 11 million and 16 million respectively. The real number of people living in these urban areas could be much higher, as more Brazilians leave the countryside for the city each day in search of jobs. As one of the world's fastest-growing cities, São Paulo's actual population might well be more than 20 million.

Rio de Janeiro

In January 1502, Portuguese explorers visited Guanabara Bay. Thinking it was a river they called it Rio de Janeiro, 'River of January'. Had they sailed in further they would have seen that this bay forms a huge natural harbour, one of the largest and safest in the world.

Rio spreads around the shores of this harbour, which has many rocky peninsulas and islands. This gives it the most spectacular setting of any city in the world. The 390 metre-high Pão de Açúcar ('Sugar Loaf') provides wonderful views over the city, mountains, bays and beaches. The symbol of Rio is the massive statue of Christ the Redeemer on the summit of Corcovado (704 metres). With arms outstretched he welcomes visitors to the city from all over the world.

People come from all over the world to enjoy Rio's Copacabana beach.

Rio is Brazil's tourist capital and has the country's busiest international airport. Visitors come mainly for the city's exciting nightlife, the marvellous beaches, such as Copacabana and Ipanema, and the annual Rio Carnival which is world famous. But not everything in this great city is fun and enjoyment. Visitors will also see that Rio has great poverty and other social problems. Many of the least fortunate are children who live on the streets, begging by day and sleeping rough at night.

São Paulo

Brazil's largest city is also the most important commercial and industrial centre in South America. Its citizens, called 'Paulistas', say that they work when

São Paulo is Brazil's financial centre.

is covered with wide avenues and overpasses with high-rise buildings stretching to the horizon in all directions. The entire city is choked with traffic and there is a huge pollution problem. It also has some of the world's largest slum and shanty settlements (favelas). In contrast some of the residential districts are among the wealthiest in Brazil. Many are the homes of foreign business-people who make São Paulo the most cosmopolitan city in Brazil. There are North American, Italian, German, Japanese, Arab, Jewish and many other ethnic districts.

Rio plays. São Paulo's growth began with coffee, and since the 19th century the city has attracted business people from all over Brazil and the world. Sprawling industrial suburbs surround the city, especially towards Santos, its port.

Hardly anything is left of old São Paulo, which was founded by Portuguese Jesuit priests in 1554. The downtown area today

Brazil's largest cities
(official population size in millions)

São Paulo	16.2
Rio de Janeiro	11.2
Belo Horizonte	3.1
Pôrto Alegre	2.6
Recife	2.5
Salvador	2.1
Fortaleza	2.0
Brasília	1.9

Brasília

In 1960 Brasília replaced Rio de Janeiro as Brazil's national capital, making it one of the world's newest capital cities. Its construction began in 1956. The site chosen was 1000 kilometres north-west of Rio, on the empty plateau land of Goiás State. It was part of an experiment to attract people away from Brazil's crowded coastal areas.

Brasília's main architect-planners were Lúcio Costa and Oscar Niemeyer. They designed daringly modern buildings, such as the Metropolitan Cathedral (see page 29), the Presidential Palace and the National Congress.

Mansions and slums

Many who move to the cities in search of work find it difficult to get jobs. They are forced to shine shoes, sell lottery tickets, run errands and even sort through rubbish to earn money. This is not enough to pay the rent for a house or flat. Instead they become 'squatters', living in shanty-towns on land they do not have a legal right to. Here conditions are often worse than those they left behind.

Favelas

Brazil's shanty-towns are called 'favelas', and the people who live in them, 'favelados'. There are many thousands of such people in every large city.

Many Brazilians live in these city 'favelas' where they encounter poverty and disease.

Favela homes are little more than shacks. They are built from any available material - wood, corrugated iron, plastic sheets, blankets, cardboard and thatch. Inside are one or two small rooms where the family lives, eats and sleeps. There is no electricity, gas, running water, toilet or refuse collection. Typhoid, dysentery and other diseases are common in these insanitary and overcrowded conditions.

Rio's Rocinha Favela

Some of the oldest and largest favelas are in Rio. There are nearly 500 of them, and they are growing all the time. Many spread up the hillsides, overlooking the rich neighbourhoods of Copacabana and Ipanema. On these steep slopes heavy rainfall causes landslides, which carry the favela homes downhill. There have been many losses of life.

No one knows how many people live in Rocinha, South America's largest favela. There might be 60,000 favelados, or twice that number. Although health and social conditions are deplorable Rocinha is lucky, as the Rio municipality has given it electricity and running water, but no sewage disposal. There are also shops, a bank, cafe-bars and a job centre. Like many favelas, it is still a district of drug-selling and gang violence.

The mansions

All Brazilian cities have districts where rich people live. Rio's Ipanema beachfront is lined with luxurious apartments, and São Paulo's Morumbi neighbourhood has California-styled mansions. With large gardens and swimming pools, they are protected by high security walls. They are the homes of Brazil's political, industrial and land-owning rulers. They own expensive cars, have servants and probably have other homes in the countryside, or abroad. These people make up the richest 10 per cent of Brazil's population. They also account for over 50 per cent of the country's income.

The apartment blocks

In huge contrast to the mansions are the inner city housing areas. Most are high-rise apartment blocks. Many people live

Multi-storey housing blocks are common in all large Brazilian cities.

huddled together in noisy and polluted neighbourhoods. Here again there is much crime and violence. Even so, they are far better living areas than the favelas. The worst of Brazil's living standards are to be found among the people of the streets. Many of these are children (see page 17). This is the country's biggest social problem.

Homes in the countryside

Although many people are leaving for the cities, Brazil is still a country of farming villages and small market towns. The most attractive are those dating from colonial times. The Portuguese-style village house is of two or three rooms, built round a courtyard. This opens on to a cobbled street, leading to a central square and the church. Close by is the old colonial mansion, the sobrado, where the family might still own the village and its land.

There have been many important changes. Now more farmers own their land. New roads and electricity have also improved rural life. But there are not enough improvements to stop people moving from Brazil's countryside to the cities.

Health, food and education

For many Brazilians medical care is poor. Those who can afford it join private health services. But for the rest there are not enough doctors, hospitals and medicines for those who are ill. A large number of babies die soon after birth. This death rate is highest in the northeast, and in the urban slums of the large southern cities.

A travelling medical team awaiting patients

Throughout the country young and old fall victims to many infectious diseases. Most are caused by drinking dirty water, and by poor sewage disposal. In Amazonia yellow fever, malaria and other tropical diseases are common. Travelling bus clinics and river-boat hospitals provide immunization and other medical help.

Food and diet

Poverty and hunger are other reasons for the low health standard. Over half the people in Brazil are poorly fed. This means they catch diseases more easily.

Beans, rice and manioc are the basic ingredients in Brazilian food. But such a large country has many food dishes and styles of cooking. In the northeast a lot of fish is eaten and recipes use different spices, palm oil, fruits and vegetables. Further south there is more pork, beef and lamb. This is the home of 'Feijoada', Brazil's national dish.

Feijoada

This is a type of stew, made from black beans and different kinds of meats. It is simmered for a long time, along with an assortment of vegetables and other ingredients.

Feijoada was originally made from leftovers to feed the slaves. Today it is eaten by rich and poor alike. It is served with side dishes of rice, shredded kale, toasted manioc root and sliced oranges. Some like it with a hot pepper sauce. Rio's Feijoada is said to be the best.

Brazilians are also fond of snacks. All large cities have their fast-food places selling pizzas, hamburgers and kebabs. There are also stalls selling 'Salgadinhas', very spicy pasties filled with cheese, shrimp, chicken or mincemeat.

Going to school

For many Brazilian children this is a luxury. The best schools are the private, fee-paying ones. Their pupils usually go on to secondary and university education. The state schools, which are free, are overcrowded, lack money and equipment, and have a shortage of teachers.

Some of these children will probably leave school before they learn to read or write.

In state schools, few children complete their elementary education. Children need to work to help support their poor families. Many leave school unable to read and write. At present Brazil's illiteracy rate, for young and old, is one of the highest in the world. Some of the main cities have night schools which teach, feed and medically help children. The 'Universidado Alberta' (Open University) began its radio and television programmes in 1989. Part of its task is to reduce illiteracy and give the people of Brazil a better chance to learn.

Street jobs
Selling things
Washing cars
Carrying shopping
Sorting out garbage
Running errands
Singing and dancing
Shining shoes
Telling fortunes
Keeping places in queues
Begging
Stealing (and other crimes)

The 'Deserted Ones'
It is said there are 12 million Brazilian children living without parents. Thousands of them, many under 10 years of age, live on city streets. They are called 'abandonados', the deserted ones.

They survive as best they can, and few go to school. Life is very dangerous for them. They are often attacked, put in prison, and many have been murdered.

Most are very proud children who do all sorts of dirty jobs, just to survive. Some try to save money for a better life.

Farming, forestry and fishing

About one quarter of all Brazilians depend on farming for a living. A huge variety of crops are grown, some only for family needs, others for export. As it is mainly a tropical country, there are many exotic fruits, vegetables and other crops. The best place to see them is in the lively local market-places.

Coffee

This is Brazil's most important crop and main agricultural export. São Paulo and Paraná are the chief coffee growing states. Their climate and rich soil, called 'terra roxa', suit the coffee bush. During the 19th century, many Europeans came to work on the large coffee 'fazendas' (plantation estates). Their owners grew rich, and the coffee trade led to the rapid growth of São Paulo city, and Santos. This is still the world's largest coffee shipping port.

Coffee plantations made São Paulo rich.

Brazilians drink a lot of coffee, but much of it also goes to the USA. Some of it is mixed with other varieties to make instant coffee, on sale in supermarkets throughout the world. In 1975 severe frost ruined the coffee harvest, causing a big rise in world coffee prices. The 'Brazilian Coffee Institute' now controls the amount of coffee grown and exported each year.

Other plantation crops

Sugar-cane was Brazil's first important export crop. It is still grown on plantations in the northeast and, nowadays, in the southeast. All the time production is increasing, as Brazil uses sugar to make fuel (see page 21).

Cocoa, used in chocolate and drinks, is grown in the State of Bahía. In October a lively 'Cocoa Festival' takes place in Salvador. In the southeast there are large cotton plantations, and wheat and rice are important field crops in the State of Rio Grande do Sul.

Fruits and nuts

Almost every kind of fruit is grown in Brazil, from tropical varieties to temperate ones. Pineapple, banana, passion fruit and mango come from Amazonia, as well as nuts such as cashew, peanut, brazil nut, and kola nut (used in Coca Cola). Spices

Timber is one of Brazil's main natural resources.

Timber

Brazil has some of the world's largest supplies of timber. In Amazonia there are over 400 types of hardwood, including those used to make quality furniture. Other hardwood forests are along the Atlantic coast. In the south there are forests of pine, and other softwoods, grown for paper and pulp industries.

There is now a limit to the number of hardwood trees that can be cut. Instead of making furniture from solid wood, a thin sheet of expensive hardwood (a veneer) is stuck on to a cheaper material. But there are still many people cutting trees without any thought of conservation.

include chillies, cayenne and black peppers, nutmeg, cloves, vanilla, cinnamon and tumeric.

In the south region enormous amounts of citrus fruits are grown. Brazil is the world's largest producer and exporter of oranges and orange juice. Here there are also large areas growing vines. Grape growing and wine production has long been in the hands of German, Italian and other European colonists.

Livestock

The best beef and hogs come from the south, where the temperate grasslands resemble the 'pampas' of Uruguay and Argentina. In the Brazilian Highlands the pasture lands are called 'campos'. They are drier and poorer, and many cattle are raised only for their hides. Large areas of rainforest have been cleared for cattle ranches. Most of the beef is sold to the large international hamburger companies. This is one of Brazil's most wasteful forms of agriculture. Not only is forest flora and fauna destroyed, the soil is poor and supports few cattle over a large area.

Fishing

Fishing, both sea and freshwater, has always been important in Brazil. The Brazilian coastline extends for 7,326 kilometres, with an offshore fishing limit of 320 kilometres. Tuna is found along the entire coast and this, together with other important fish stocks, is now being more carefully managed. The northeast is the country's most important fishing region. The great variety of the local catch can be seen in the huge fish markets of Salvador, Recife and Fortaleza. Further north, at the

mouth of the Amazon, is the world's largest shrimp bank.

Industry and power

Brazil has some of the world's largest supplies of mineral ores. These include iron, tin, bauxite (used to make aluminium), copper, manganese, nickel, uranium, tungsten and niobium (used for steel alloys). It also has rich reserves of precious metals and stones, such as diamonds, amethyst and topazes. In the 1980s another area of gold was discovered in the Serra Pelado, a mountain range in Pará State. Thousands of 'garimpeiros' (gold panners) have turned it into the world's largest gold mine.

Brazil has many rich deposits of iron ore.

Minas Gerais

Meaning 'General Mines', this is Brazil's chief mining State. At the end of the 17th century prospectors moved in from the coast in search of gold and diamonds. Today, the main mineral is iron ore, found in the mountains to the southeast of Belo Horizonte, the State capital. Many rugged peaks, such as Itabirito, are made almost entirely of iron ore. This makes it one of the world's richest reserves. Other important iron ore supplies are in the States of Pará and Mato Grosso do Sul.

Steel, cars and aircraft

Based on its iron ore, Brazil has many large, integrated steel plants, which are government owned. It is the world's 7th most important producer of steel. Most of it is used in the country's heavy

This woman is looking for emeralds.

An aeroplane on the factory assembly-line

manufacturing industries, such as shipbuilding, railway stock, cars and other vehicles, and aircraft. It is also used in the canning industry, for Brazil's many food and drink products.

Brazil's car industry is one of the largest in the world. Volkswagen, General Motors and Ford are located in São Paulo, and Fiat in Belo Horizonte. Cars are exported to other Latin American countries, the United States, Africa and the Middle East. Brazil has built a car that runs on alcohol (see below).

Power and energy

Whatever else Brazil may have, it is short of fossil fuels – coal, natural gas and oil. Some coal is mined near Pôrto Alegre, but coke, in exchange for iron ore is imported from the United States. Oil is the biggest problem as the country produces only one-fifth of its needs. The search is on for new coal and oil supplies. New sources of oil have been discovered in the Manaus area.

But Brazil has no shortage of running water. Many large hydro-electric schemes have been built to increase the country's energy supply. The massive dam at Itaipú, on the Paraná River (see box) is one of the world's largest water energy projects.

The Itaipú Dam
Completed in 1982, this dam is located on the Brazil-Paraguay border, 720 kilometres west of São Paulo. Its massive artificial lake drowned the homes of 200,000 people. It also submerged the Guira Falls, 190 kilometres upstream. Its body of water was once twelve times greater than Africa's Victoria Falls.

Energy farming

Through photosynthesis, plants convert energy into chemical form. Experiments in Brazil show that sugar gives the best energy yield. One tonne of sugar provides about 70 litres of alcohol. This is mixed with petrol (gasoline) to make 'gasohol', which powers over five million Brazilian cars. Other plants are being tested for their energy value, including manioc, sorghum and sweet potato.

Transport and tourism

The Brazilian bus

The country's favourite form of travel is the bus, which links all towns and cities, and most villages. There are hundreds of private companies and journeys are cheap.

The main bus stations, called 'rodoviarias', are usually found on the outskirts of towns. They are noisy and colourful places, with many people selling food, drink and other items for the journey. Some of Brazil's bus journeys last for several days and nights.

New roads

Most of Brazil's main roads and motorways are in the southeast region, but parts of the south, centre west and northeast also have modern networks. Motorways link São Paulo, Rio, Belo Horizonte and Brasília. The busiest stretch of all is between São Paulo and the port of Santos.

The Trans-Amazonian Highway cuts through hundreds of miles of forested areas.

Many new highways have been built across the country and others are under construction. The famous Trans-Amazon Highway stretches from Recife to the Peruvian border. It is part of Brazil's plan to attract people into the Amazon from the dry and poor northeast. Together with other highways it has damaged parts of the forest and the lives of the Indians.

Traffic problems

Huge traffic problems occur in all of Brazil's large cities. Streets are constantly clogged with buses, taxis, cars and lorries, and exhaust fumes pollute the air. In São Paulo industry and traffic fumes combine to make it one of the world's most polluted cities.

Another problem is driving standards. Brazil has the world's highest record of fatal road accidents, in the cities and the countryside. Plans to extend the underground (metro) in Rio, São Paulo and other places will, hopefully, reduce the number of cars.

Plane, boat and train

Because of its size, Brazil relies a great deal on air travel. There are airstrips everywhere, and all main cities have airports. The busiest domestic route is between São Paulo and Rio, where a

Boat passengers relax in hammocks.

Tourism

Except in places like Rio and Salvador, the tourist industry in Brazil is not well-developed. Most foreign visitors are business people who stay in São Paulo. The country has a wealth of tourist attractions which the Brazilian National Tourist Board (Embratur) is trying to make popular. New hotels and other facilities have been built in the northeast, in parts of Amazonia and in the colonial towns of the southeast. Many people believe that tourism will solve most of Brazil's social and economic problems. Others are not so sure, pointing out that this has not been the case in the Caribbean islands or Mexico.

shuttle service operates. These are also Brazil's main international airports. As well as the main airlines (Varig-Cruzeir, Vasp and Transbrazil), there are many smaller companies, especially in Amazonia. Here they operate air-taxi services, known as 'teco-teco flights', to remote areas.

Another means of Amazonian travel is by boat, but this is slow and often tough-going. The main river is navigable to ocean-going ships as far as Iquitos in Peru. Along the river and its tributaries are ferryboat terminals (hidroviárias).

Great railway journeys

Curitiba – Paranaguá (Paraná State)
110 kms of spectacular mountain scenery
Ouro Preto – Mariana (Minas Gerais State)
20 kms through Brazil's colonial countryside
Pôrto Velho – Cachoeria de Teotônia (Rondonia State)
20 kms of tropical scenery
Rio de Janeiro – São Paulo (9 hours)
Luxury night train with sleeper, diner car and room service

Except for the busy commuter railways of the cities, trains are not very popular in Brazil. Most of the railways were built in the 19th century to carry minerals and crops to the ports. Many passenger lines have been closed but a few journeys still operate for the tourist. Some of these are mountain lines still using steam power.

Tourists visiting Brazil can enjoy a journey by steam train.

Religion and festivals

Brazil's many different peoples have given the country a great mixture of religions. Roman Catholicism is the main official religion, but many Brazilians practise a number of other faiths. As well as Christian saints, it is common for Indian idols and African gods to be included in their worship and prayers.

Indian beliefs

The early Portuguese settlers brought Christianity to Brazil. Among them were Jesuit priests and other missionaries. They regarded the native Indians as 'savages' and 'heathens'. On many occasions they brutally forced them to accept Christianity, killing those who refused.

A ceremony called 'Washing the church steps'

The Indians believe that all natural things, such as trees, water, earth and wind have spirits and souls. This helps them to properly care for their environment and their ancestors. This belief is called 'animism' and is found among many tribal peoples throughout the world. Other Brazilians, even in the cities, believe in spirits and often use strong, drugged drink as part of their ceremonies.

Church and saints

Brazil claims to have the largest Catholic population of any country in the world. Every village and town district has its church, and many are large and beautiful buildings. Some of the oldest and richest churches are in the northeast, and in the state of Minas Gerais. Here the colonial town of Ouro Preto has been made a UNESCO World Cultural Heritage centre. Its churches have priceless paintings, 'azulejos' (Portuguese tile pictures), gilded carvings and holy statues decorated with precious stones.

Each local church has its Dia de Festa, the celebration of its patron saint. The saint's statue or picture is carried through the streets in a procession, led by a band. After mass, the festival turns to eating, drinking and dancing.

Brazilian churches are often decorated in gold and precious stones.

Brazil also has national religious days. October 12 is one holiday in honour of the country's patron saint, Our Lady of the Conception. Each year millions of pilgrims visit her statue in the church on the Rio-São Paulo highway.

Afro-Brazilian cults

Today in Brazil, the Catholic religion is not as strong as it once was. Congregations are dwindling and churches are closing, because there is not enough money to pay the priest. Many people are joining the Afro-Brazilian religions instead.

The slaves brought from Africa were not allowed by the Portuguese to practise their religions. To overcome this problem they adapted their beliefs and worship to those of the Catholic church. Even their gods, the 'Orixás', were given the names of Christian saints. This religion is 'Candomblé', which means 'to dance in the honour of the gods'. The music, rites and language are similar to West African religions. There are many followers throughout Brazil, but the northeast is the main Candomblé region. February 2 is one of its important days, the Festival of Lemanjá (Queen of the Seas) when Brazilians take to the sea and dance in her honour. It is said that Lemanjá has many of the characteristics of the Virgin Mary. Candomblé priests are respected members of their local communities.

Brazil's other holidays

Most Brazilian holidays are religious ones, except for Labour Day (May 1), Republic Day (November 15) and Independence Day (September 7). Independence Day celebrates Tiradentes, who fought for Brazil's freedom from Portugal and was executed in 1789. His dream of independence did not come true until a century later.

The Brazilian carnival has its origins in the Roman Catholic period leading up to Lent and Holy Week. Carnival is a time for enjoyment and Rio has the most famous and spectacular carnival in the world (see page 27).

Sports and pastimes

Football

Football is very popular in Brazil. All towns and most large villages have a football team, and there are always league matches. Children play the game in the streets, on beaches, in parks and just about anywhere. This type of football has slightly different rules and is called 'pelado'.

In the cities thousands of fans support their teams in the massive stadiums. Rio's Maracaña Stadium has room for 200,000 spectators. It was built in 1950 when Brazil hosted the World Cup. São Paulo and Belo Horizonte also have huge football grounds. It is said that, altogether, Brazil's stadiums can hold 4 million people.

Going to a big football match is an exciting occasion. The crowd wave flags, throw tickertape, honk horns, beat drums and roar their approval (or otherwise) to their teams. It is a noisy, family occasion, and usually there is little trouble or violence. During the World Cup, Brazil comes to a halt, as everyone watches the cup matches on television.

Other spectator sports

Brazilians love the excitement of speed and enjoy watching motor racing. São Paulo and Rio have world famous Grand Prix circuits which attract thousands of spectators. However, motor racing is also a very dangerous sport and in April 1994 one of Brazil's greatest champions, Ayrton Senna, was killed in a race.

The Grand Prix is a popular event.

Brazil's football king

Brazil won the World Cup in 1958, 1962 1970 and 1994. The most famous player was Edson Arantes do Nascimento. He known to everyone in Brazil as Pelé, because of his skill as a young boy at playing pelada. In 1974, he retired from professional football, after a career lasting 18 years. In all his games he scored more than 1,200 goals. In 1969 he dedicated his 1000th goal to the 'Children of Brazil'. Pelé has been in films, on television, and books have been written about him. In Brazil he is a national hero called 'O Rei' ('The King').

Capoeira wrestling dates from the days of slavery

A unique Brazilian sport is Capoeira. It is a mixture of martial art and dance, with African-style music. Slaves were not allowed to train, fight or keep fit, so they disguised this sport, a kind of wrestling, as an acrobatic dance.

Television

As well as sport, Brazilians love watching soap operas on television. Just about everyone gets involved with the characters and storylines. Called telenovelas, they are shown at peak viewing time. Most are about the problems of middle-class city families, a kind of Brazilian 'Neighbours'. It is rude to telephone or visit during telenovela time.

In many parts of Brazil television is the only form of entertainment, but not everyone can afford it. Villagers turn up at the local cafe-bar to watch their favourite programmes. There is a large choice as Brazil has many TV stations. 'Globo' and 'Bandeirantes' are the biggest, and their programmes are nationwide, reaching most parts of the country.

Popular music and dance

Music is very important to the Brazilian people. Their music is a mixture of many different styles, especially Portuguese (and Spanish), African, native Indian and North American. The 1930s is called the 'Golden Age' of Brazilian music.

Many Latin American dances come from Brazil, including the 'Bossa-Nova' and the 'Lambada'. But the most famous is the 'Samba', which is the music of the Rio and other carnivals. Rio has hundreds of 'Samba Schools', one for each neighbourhood taking part in the annual carnival. They rehearse all year long, composing an original samba song, and making costumes for the spectacular parade. The Rio carnival is one of the world's greatest free shows.

Samba bands in colourful costumes lead each float in the Rio carnival.

Arts and culture

Indian Art

Because of its mixture of peoples, Brazil has a great variety of arts and handicrafts. The Indians make many colourful products, some of them for religious purposes. The Indians use forest products, such as grasses, leaves and fibres to make baskets, bags and blankets. The rich colours come from plant and other natural dyes. Some are skilled potters and also make ceramic figurines, which are painted. The colourful plumage of forest birds is used for headdresses, capes and necklaces. These are part of the special costumes for religious and other occasions.

Brightly-coloured feathers are an important part of Indian ceremonial costume.

Artists

Other than the Indians, Brazil's first artists were the colonial missionaries. They built churches and decorated them in Europe's Baroque style. When gold was discovered in the 18th century many beautiful works of art were created. Brazil's most famous artist and architect of this time was Antônio Francisco Lisboa, also known as Aleijadinho. Many of his statues and other masterpieces can be seen in the old colonial churches.

The best-known modern Brazilian artist is Candido Portinari. Most of his paintings are of Brazil and its people. His mural 'War and Peace' is in the United Nations building in New York.

Architecture

A number of places in Brazil have been made world heritage centres by UNESCO. This is because of their outstanding architecture. Representing the colonial period is the town of Olinda, in Pernambuco State. Its beautiful churches, palaces and colonial homes date from the 16th and 17th centuries. Here nothing can be altered or painted without government permission. Ouro Preto in Minas Gerais State is another protected colonial town, and so is the old centre of Salvador.

Downtown Brasília is also a UNESCO heritage centre, in this case for its modern architecture. One of its unusual buildings is the concrete and glass cathedral which resembles Christ's own crown of thorns.

Concerts and films

As well as its huge variety of popular music, Brazil's cities have large halls for orchestral concerts and theatrical performances. In July an important music festival takes place at Campos do Jordão,

The 'crown of thorns' cathedral in Brasília

a mountain resort in São Paulo State. This is a South American equivalent of the Salzburg and Edinburgh festivals, at least as far as classical music is concerned.

Another important cultural occasion is 'FestRio', the international film festival held each September in Rio de Janeiro. Brazil's film industry is growing all the time, and a number of films have won awards at Cannes and other world film festivals.

Opera in the forest

The 'Teatro Amazonas' is the famous opera house built in Manaus during the rubber boom. The architect was Domenico de Angelis, who used cast-iron structures from Britain, marble and porcelain from Italy and chandeliers and mirrors from France. Famous opera stars from all over the world came to sing at Manaus. One story goes that the audience were so rich, they threw diamonds on stage instead of flowers. Opera and ballet performances are still held throughout the year.

Medicines

The Amazonian Indians know how useful forest plants can be as medicines. Some of their knowledge has been passed on to us. In fact, one in four of the ingredients found in a chemist come from the leaves, roots, fruits, barks and other natural selva products. Yet much of Amazonia is still unexplored. New plants and insects are found all the time. They might be clues to curing the world's greatest diseases.

Brazil and the world

Trade and investment

Since the 1960s Brazil has seen tremendous economic changes. Many foreign countries have invested in its motor vehicle, chemical and pharmaceutical industries, as well as in farming. Attracted by Brazil's resources and supply of cheap labour, these 'multinationals' account for a large part of the country's production and exports. Brazil's main trading links are with the EC, USA, Latin America, Japan and the Middle East. This partly accounts for the cosmopolitan business districts in São Paulo and other cities. Recently, trade with Angola and other old Portuguese colonies has been increasing.

A busy scene in central São Paulo

Modern financial districts can be seen in all large Brazilian cities.

The country's debt

Brazil owes many hundreds of millions of pounds to foreign banks. Huge amounts were borrowed when the military governed the country between 1964 and 1985. This money was needed for the great development projects, such as new roads, dams and the building of Brasília. All were part of the plan to modernise Brazil, and the generals also encouraged the multinational firms to invest in the country. Much of the money was wasted, and today Brazil is the world's biggest debtor. Another problem is the huge rise in prices, which makes the condition of the poor much worse. Democracy was fully restored in 1990, but the present government is still left with a huge financial problem.

The Rio Summit

Brazil's massive size and rich natural resources make it important to the entire world. In June 1992, a conference on the global environment was held in Rio de Janeiro. It was attended by representatives from most countries. They discussed how the environment might be best protected from pollution and similar damage. Other topics included population increase and birth control, health and disease, and poverty.

The Rio Summit reminded us all of the dangers threatening the Brazilian rainforest.

The 'tree of life' at the Rio Summit.

The conference talked about environments such as Amazonia. As well as destroying flora, fauna and native life, the destruction of forest has worldwide results. The smoke from burning vast forest areas contributes to the 'greenhouse effect'. The fewer trees there are in the world to absorb carbon dioxide, the faster the greenhouse effect and 'global warming'. The conference made it clear that many countries are responsible for what is happening in Amazonia.

Index and summary

Area	8,511,965 square kilometres
Population	155 million (approx)
Capital city	Brasília (Federal District)
Main cities	São Paulo, Rio de Janeiro, Belo Horizonte, Pôrto Alegre, Recife, Salvador, Fortaleza, Brasília (capital), Curitiba, Belém, Goiana, Manaus
Regions	North, Northeast, Centre West, Southeast, South
States	North: Amazonas, Acre, Rondônia, Pará, Roraima, Amapá
	Northeast: Maranhão, Piauí, Ceará, Rio Grande do Norte, Paraíba, Pernambuco, Alagoas, Sergipe, Bahia
	Centre West: Tocantins, Goiás, Mato Grosso, Mato Grosso do Sul
	Southeast: Minas Gerais, Espirito Santo, Rio de Janeiro, São Paulo
	South: Paraná, Santa Catarina, Rio Grande do Sul
Main exports	Iron ore, steel products, machine parts, cars, aircraft, coffee, cocoa, citrus fruits, other raw materials
Longest river	The Amazon and its tributaries
Highest mountain	Pico da Bandeira (2890 metres), Espirito Santo State
Languages	Portuguese, Indian languages, and many communities speaking immigrant tongues
Currency	In July 1994 Brazil's currency was changed from the cruzeiro to the real.
National airlines	Varig-Cruzeiro, Vasp and Transbrazil